White Spirit Bear

D0784981

Dedicated to those who make a difference
to preserve all wildlife and especially to **Kodie**,
that famous and much loved Kermode of Terrace,
British Columbia, Canada.

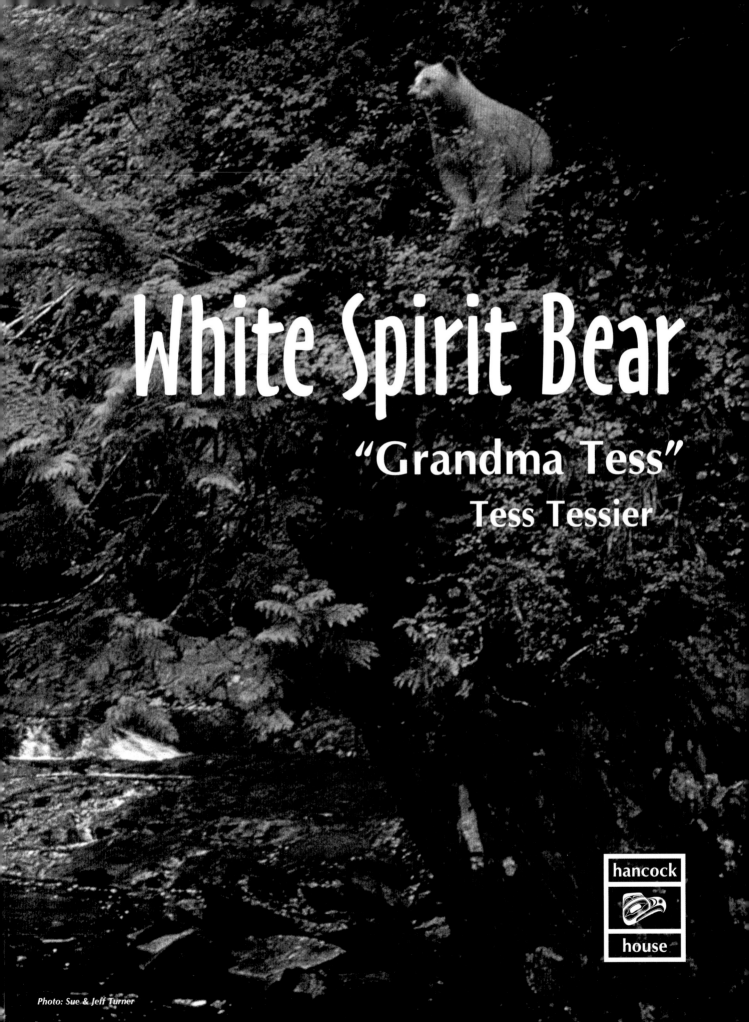

White Spirit Bear

"Grandma Tess"

Tess Tessier

hancock
house

ISBN 0-88839-462-4 (bound)
ISBN 0-88839-475-6 (pbk.)
Copyright © 2000 Tess Tessier

Second soft cover printing 2005

Cataloging in Publication Data
Tessier, Tess, 1925–
    White spirit bear

    ISBN 0-88839-462-4 (bound) — ISBN 0-88839-475-6 (pbk.)

    1. Bears—British Columbia—Pacific Coast—Juvenile literature. I. Title.
QL737.C27T47 2000   j599.78   C99-911023-3

Photographers
R. D. Anderson
Dennis Beaudette
Roger Bourgoin
Kyla Campbell
Anthony Carter
Gordon Clent
Heather Conn, Kermode Creations
Department of Fisheries and Oceans
Adrian Dorst
Barry English
Gary Gray
Joe Haits
David Hancock
Bill Henderson
Peter Jess
Steven Kazlowski
Myron Kozak
Dave Lockhart
Joe Mandur - Front Cover
Erica Mallam, Valhalla Wilderness Society
Mavis Mark
Matson's Laboratory
David McCrory
Wayne McCrory, Valhalla Wilderness Society
Michael Neugebauer
Frank Ridler
John Roders
Charlie Russell, Lenticular Productions Ltd.
Deloras Smith
Sue and Jeff Turner, River Road Films Ltd.
Herb Yehl

Illustrators
Freda Diesing, White Bear Native Design
Susan Im Baumgarten, pp. 5, 32, 43
Liz Mitten Ryan
Anne Sherrod

Acknowledgments
Alcan Smelters
Bank of Montreal
Bank of Nova Scotia
16-37 Community Future
    & Business Development Center
Copperside Stores
Lou & Cathy Elorza
Kitselas First Nation
Kitsumkalum First Nation
Northern Savings Credit Union
Royal Bank
Skeena Broadcasters
Valhalla Wilderness Society
Western Canada Wilderness Committee

Edited by Nancy Miller
Book and cover design by Ingrid Luters
Production by Ingrid Luters and Nancy Miller

Printed in South Korea—PACOM

Terrace, British Columbia, Canada adopts White Spirit Bear

A high percentage of the black bears around the city of Terrace B.C. are white coated.

The city of Terrace is proud of this natural heritage and has adopted this rare white Kermode bear as its official emblem. These unique bears have a special place of honor among all the people of northwestern British Columbia.

Published simultaneously in Canada and the United States by

HANCOCK HOUSE PUBLISHERS LTD.
19313 Zero Avenue, Surrey, B.C. Canada V3S 9R9
(604) 538-1114   Fax (604) 538-2262

HANCOCK HOUSE PUBLISHERS
1431 Harrison Avenue, Blaine, WA U.S.A. 98230-5005
(604) 538-1114   Fax (604) 538-2262

Website: www.hancockhouse.com • *Email:* sales@hancockhouse.com

Contents

About the Author

An educator, writer and adventuress, Tess Tessier lives by the philosophies of peace, caring and sharing. To spread her message of harmonious living, Grandma Tess and her furry friends tour the country in their 1973 GMC fuchsia, purple and turquoise "home on wheels" visiting schools.

Born in Saskatchewan, Tess grew up in an adventurous family. Her grandmother was a nurse who was sent by the Canadian government to the Arctic during the flu epidemic in the 1920s. Tess' grandparents built the Kost Trading Post in Aklavik, NWT. Her grandmother was the first woman skipper to pilot a scow (flat-bottomed barge) north on the mighty Slave, Athabasca and McKenzie Rivers, carrying supplies for the trading post. Tess' mother was the first woman jockey in Canada. Tess' adventures include being the first woman to drive solo up the Dempster Highway when it opened in 1979 in the Northwest Territories, with her furry friend Gigi (a poo-terrier from the SPCA). In 1980 Tess soloed the Mighty McKenzie River in an unsinkable Gurmman canoe with her companions Gigi and Liechein (a doberman). Tess credits her grandmother and mother with encouraging her to follow her dreams.

Photo: John Roders

Tess spent much time in the Arctic and Alaska and eventually settled on a homestead north of Terrace with her husband, seven children and Grandpa Kost. At the age of fifty, with her children grown up and her husband having passed away, Tess reevaluated her life and decided to sell her possessions. She bought a motorhome and hit the road.

Sharing the road with Tess are various furry companions, some adopted from the SPCA. Tess and her companions, The Rainbow Ambassadors, have been visiting school children for nearly twenty-five years. She has shown slide presentations in schools depicting her life in the Arctic, homesteading and a multicultural fashion show. She is currently presenting her White Spirit Bear documentary. The traveling entourage shows how we can all get along and that we must respect each other and our planet, along with the value of believing in yourself.

In *White Spirit Bear*, Tess hopes to further promote education and awareness of living in unity and harmony with our planet Earth and all its creatures. As an acknowledgment of Tess' contribution to conservation, all the photographs presented in this beautiful book have been donated by their photographers.

In the four years the author has worked on this book, she diligently researched the facts and has presented this book to the best of her knowledge and research. If there are any errors or omissions, the author apologizes.

Photo: Kyla Campbell

Foreword

For millions of years, during the course of evolution, hundreds of plant and animal species have appeared on Earth, multiplied, and then, for a variety of reasons, vanished. We all know of animals today—such as the mountain gorilla and chimpanzee, the elephant and the rhinoceros—that face extinction because of irresponsible human activity or changes in environmental conditions. Amazingly, hundreds of species of insects and plants become extinct before we can even classify them, but fortunately in modern times we are beginning to understand that all living things are connected. When we destroy a plant species, we may be depriving the world of an amazing cure for human diseases. And we know that if we destroy the forest, the desert creeps forward and the climate changes, wild animals die off because they cannot survive the harsh conditions, and humans, too, face starvation and death. Let us remember that every creature and plant is part of a web of life, each perfect, each contributing to the whole. It is up to each of us to end the destruction of our natural world before it becomes too late. Future generations will find it hard to forgive us if we fail to act. No matter what our age or where we live, it is time for every one of us to get involved and play our part.

DR. JANE GOODALL, ETHOLOGIST

Photo: Michael Neugebauer

Roots & Shoots

Roots & Shoots is the environmental and humanitarian program for youth (pre-school to university) of The Jane Goodall Institute (JGI). Its mission is to foster respect and compassion for all living things; to promote understanding of all cultures and beliefs; and to inspire each individual to take action to make the world a better place for animals, the environment and the human community.

Dr. Jane Goodall believes that the future of our planet is in the hands of the world's young people. With this in mind, Roots & Shoots was founded in 1991 in Dar es Salaam, Tanzania, East Africa. Since then it has spread to over 30 countries, and is particularly strong in Canada.

Each Roots & Shoots group needs an enthusiastic adult (often a teacher) to serve as co-ordinator. The members of the group then decide together what projects they would like to organize to address local concerns. The projects need to show care and concern in three areas: the environment, animals and the human community.

Benefits of membership include becoming part of JGI's global network, Partnerships in Understanding, receiving regular Roots & Shoots newsletters and the JGI annual World Report, and participating in Dr. Jane's Roots & Shoots Achievement Awards Program.

For more information contact:
The Jane Goodall Institute Canada
P.O. Box 477, Victoria Station
Westmount, Quebec
H3Z 2Y6

Tel: (514) 369-3384 • Fax: (514) 489-8748
E-mail: jgi@cam.org • www.janegoodall.ca
1-888-88CHIMP

Photo: Sue & Jeff Turner

Introduction

Photo: Heather Conn

White Spirit Bear

This book tells the story of a rare white subspecies of black bears living in an ancient rainforest in a remote and secluded area of the northern Pacific coast of Canada. These unique bears have an almost mystical appearance with their creamy white fur and ivory-colored claws.

Photo: Wayne McCrory

Not all white bears are polar bears!

This is the story of special bears that are little known and seldom seen. They live on the northwest coast of British Columbia.

Photo: Frances Stanley

The Bears' History

The white black bear has long been known to the Native peoples of the the Northwest coast. The tribes to the south, the Kwakiutl (pronounced kwog-ulth) people, and those to the north, the Tsimshian (pronounced sim-shan) people, attributed great prestige and respect to this unusual visitor to their land.

The Tsimshian named the bear Moksgm'ol, meaning White Bear, and he is featured in their tribal clan crests.

Photo: Joe Haits

©Freda Diesing

The bears were first seen by Native people. They gave the bears the name Moksgm'ol, which means White Bear. The bears are treated with respect and honor.

©Freda Diesing

Raven Legend

From the beginning of time, the Raven has played a big role in mythical folklore. Raven is not only a central image in aboriginal legends, but a universal figure in ancient cultures around the world.

A northwest Native legend tells that Raven, the trickster, was first snow white then transformed to black by being skillful and cunning, surviving on his wits.

White ravens are still seen along the northwest coast just as are the white spirit bears. Most white ravens, however, have pink eyes which tells us they are albinos.

Photo: Mavis Mark

Photo: Bill Henderson

One legend speaks of Raven, who went among the black bears and promised that every tenth bear cub would be born white. Raven wanted a reminder of the time when the world was pure and clean and covered with snowdrifts and ice blue glaciers. Raven promised the White Spirit Bear a life of peace in the ancient rainforest of Princess Royal Island and the nearby mainland mountains and valleys.

The Home of Spirit Bear

Today, much of the once peaceful ancient rainforest home of black and white Kermode bears has been roaded and logged but for a cluster of islands including Princess Royal Island, a largely pristine and almost magical wilderness. Here in the core of a proposed sanctuary there are an estimated 100 white-phase Kermode bears. These bears are living reminders of the innumerable animals living in the wilderness that need your commitment for their protection.

This unspoiled wilderness along the British Columbia coast also produces a large variety of spectacular species. Here deer and beaver abound, the wolf howls from mountaintop to intertidal beaches. And, interestingly, as this area has a special population of white black bears, many of the gray wolves of this area are black!

The great forests of spruce, fir and cedar produce perfect salmon rivers. The abundant salmon nourish the bears, wolves, seals, killer whales and eagles that forage the adjacent waters. Many unique plants contribute to this lush rainforest.

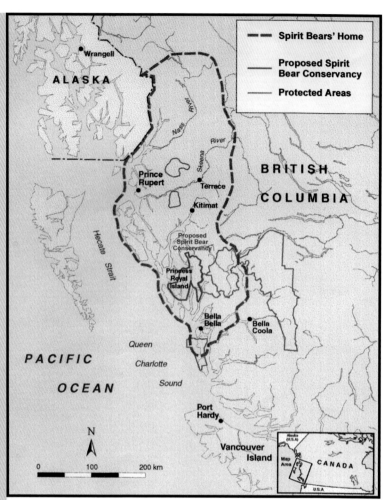

Courtesy of the Western Canada Wilderness Committee

Photo: Adrian Dorst

On an isolated island off the wooded and misty northwest coast of B.C. lives the White Spirit Bear. Thousands of years ago, when the Ice Age ended, the glaciers retreated and trees filled the coastal valleys. The old-growth rainforest of Princess Royal Island and the surrounding mainland provide a wonderful and abundant habitat for the Spirit Bears.

Photo: Adrian Dorst

Bears are dependent on huge, old trees that provide winter denning areas and large overhanging branches, which shade rivers and streams, keeping the water cool for hundreds of thousands of salmon returning to their spawning grounds. The salmon make up much of the bears' diet. Lush forest and salmon streams support the food chain, not only for Spirit Bears but also for grizzlies, deer, wolves, eagles and other wildlife.

Photo: Adrian Dorst

Photo: Adrian Dorst

Photo: Adrian Dorst

Photo: Wayne McCrory

Photo: Adrian Dorst

Photo: Steven Kazlowski

Raven's promise—a life of peace in the ancient rainforest.

What Are White Spirit Bears?

The discovery of a white bear pelt was investigated by Francis Kermode, a scientist (and later a curator) at the Provincial Museum in Victoria, B.C., along with other scientists. They traced the bearskin to the area of the Skeena and Nass Valleys along the north coast of British Columbia. The scientists declared that this was a new species, which they named *Ursus kermodei* after Francis Kermode. Later, scientists discovered that the white bears are not a separate species. They are actually white subspecies of American black bears, and their scientific name is now *Ursus americanus kermodei*. They are called Kermode Bears or Spirit Bears.

Initially, it was thought that Spirit Bears were true albino bears. Albino animals have a recessive gene that causes a lack of pigmentation in the skin, eyes and hair. But the Spirit Bears' brown eyes, black noses and ivory-colored claws confirm that they are not albinos. A recent theory suggests that the white coat is the result of a cub inheriting one recessive gene from the mother and one recessive gene from the father. This means that black-colored bears in this geographically isolated wilderness are also the *kermodei* subspecies as they can carry this recessive white gene. Presently, research is underway to investigate the possibility that a more complicated genetic mechanism, involving a mutation of the genes controlling pigmentation, is the actual cause of the white coat coloration.

Photo: Wayne McCrory

Photo: Anthony Carter

Almost 100 years ago some scientists were surprised to find a creamy white bear pelt among some black pelts brought in by a hunter. They knew it was not from a polar bear. So where did this pelt come from?

The scientists found out the bearskins came from the northwest coast of B.C. At first they thought they had discovered a new species, but later they realized that the bears are actually a subspecies of the American black bear. They named it the Kermode Bear, after the scientist who first investigated it.

Black or White or Brown?

White Spirit Bear mother with black cub

Photo: Wayne McCrory

polar bear

Photo: Peter Jess

grizzly bear

Photo: David McCrory

black bear

Photo: Steven Kazlowski

blue glacier bear

Photo: Gary Gray

brown bear

Photo: Dave Lockhart

cinnamon bear

Photo: David Hancock

Spirit Bears are black bears in which about one in ten is born with white fur. A white or a black mother bear can have all black or all white cubs, or cubs of both colors in the same litter. American black bears can be found in a range of colors. As well as black, they can be various shades of brown, and there are rarer hues such as orange, chestnut red, yellow and blue-gray (also known as glacier bear). It has been said that there are rare colorations such as pinto, a mixture of white, black and cinnamon, and pied, black and white.

Bear Cubs

The bears usually mate in May and June; however, the fertilized egg does not get established and begin to grow in the womb until fall. This is called delayed implantation. The delay ensures the cubs are born when the mother is hibernating in a den. Here, they are protected from harsh winter snows and icy winds.

The cubs are about twenty centimeters (8 in.) long when they are born, and they weigh from 225 to 450 grams (1/2 to 1 lb.); they are about the size of a kitten. Cubs are born with blue-gray eyes, which change to brown in four to six months. Newborn cubs remain alert and active, and curl or snuggle next to their mother throughout the hibernation period.

The mother provides very rich milk, which the cubs nurse on for three or four months while she is hibernating. When they leave the den, the mother bear sits in an upright position while nursing. The cubs make low, murmuring sounds and will whimper like children in distress. The cubs continue to nurse for up to a year after hibernation ends. Cubs become independent at about one and a half years old. This means mother and cubs can spend two winters in the den together. The bears to the right are brother and sister yearling cubs.

Photos: Dennis Beaudette

Although bears mate in the spring, the babies do not develop inside the mother's body until autumn. This helps to ensure the survival of both the mother and the cub. Cubs are usually born in January or February, in the warm protection of a den, while the mother is still hibernating.

Female black bears usually give birth to twins rather than triplets or single cubs. But they can have as many as four cubs. Older, heavier mothers tend to have larger litters.

The cubs get nourishment from their mother's milk and emerge from the den in the warmth of spring ready to explore their new world.

There is a strong bond between a mother bear and her cubs. She gives all her natural tendencies of nursing, warmth and snuggling, as well as discipline, such as a growl or swat from her paw to her young. Cubs are very obedient to their mothers. If alarmed, a mother bear will give a deep *awhoof* sound, warning her cubs to scamper up the nearest tree. Never very far away, she will give a few simple grunts to come down.

The cubs usually become independent from their mother between seventeen and eighteen months of age. The mothers and fathers live apart except during the brief mating period. Male bears are not involved in rearing their offspring and can be a predator on young cubs.

Photos: Wayne McCrory

Cubs are truly explorers. Once outside the den, life is full of surprises. Everything they see, smell or touch is a new experience. They can be seen sticking their noses in every nook and cranny, and chasing birds and butterflies. Cubs will mimic their mother in everything she does, learning much of their behavior from her.

Cubs' favorite pastimes are wrestling, exchanging bear hugs and playing tag. They like to roll topsy-turvy, somersaulting and cart-wheeling over each other. They sometimes roll down a hill, ending up in a tangle of fur and paws. All this play develops skills and strength for the time that they will fend for themselves in the forest.

Adult Bears

Photo: Bill Henderson

1293
This Douglas-fir
begins to grow.

Photo: David Hancock

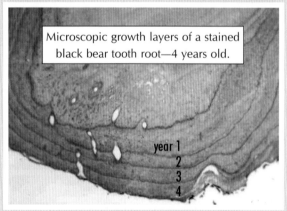

Microscopic growth layers of a stained
black bear tooth root—4 years old.

year 1
2
3
4

Photo: Matson's Laboratory

Bears' teeth, tree rings and even salmon scales show annual growth rings that can
be counted to accurately determine age.

Scientists are able to tell the age of a bear by cutting a cross-section of a tooth and counting the rings—just like counting the rings of a tree to see how old it is.

Bears have forty-two teeth. Some teeth are flat for chewing vegetation, others are sharp for tearing meat.

Bears can live for twenty years or more.

A black or white adult male bear will weigh about 150 kilograms (330 pounds), while a female weighs about 100 kilograms (220 pounds). They are usually full grown after four years. Their body length is about one and one half meters (five feet), but when they stand up on their hind legs they can be about two and one half meters (eight feet tall).

Photo: Herb Yehl

Photos: Gordon Clent

Bear Behavior

Photos: Wayne McCrory

Spirit Bears behave in much the same way as other bears. They respond to their environment—finding food, defending a territory, choosing a mate or rearing young.

Native people called them "bear people." Bears stand on the soles and heels of their feet as humans do and they will walk upright for short distances. When bears stand, it is usually to get a better look around and to sniff the air for intruders. Bears have a highly developed sense of smell. They are much more dependent on this sense, rather than their eyes or ears, for identification of other animals, food sources and danger.

Bears will stand with their backs against a tree and rub back and forth, scratching and shedding their winter coats.

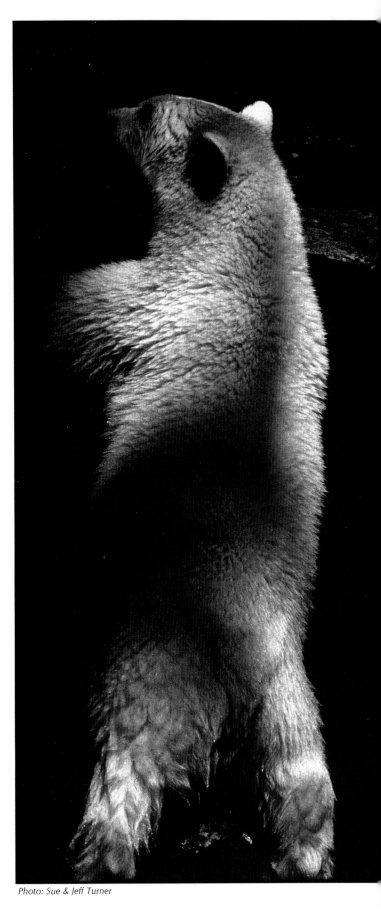

Photo: Wayne McCrory

Photo: Sue & Jeff Turner

Photo: Roger Bourgoin

Black bears are good swimmers and excellent tree climbers. Grizzlies and polar bears do not climb trees.

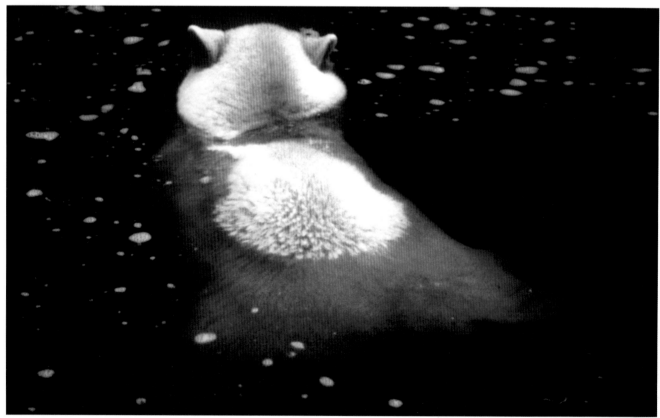

Photo: Sue & Jeff Turner

The language of bears includes both body and vocal signals. Each position or sound sends a specific message to other bears. A sign of aggression may be shown by a lowered head position, flattened ears, head swung back and forth, or vocal sounds, such as grunts, snorts, bellowing or clicks made by opening and closing their mouths. All bears, including Spirit Bears, can be dangerous and should be given plenty of room and treated with respect.

The Bears' Diet

In spring, bears feed on sedges, grasslike plants found near wet ground or water. Grasses, skunk cabbage, roots and insects also constitute a large part of their spring diet. Searching for food takes up much of a bear's time.

Wildflowers become summer treats, while wild berries become an important food source at this time. Surprisingly, the bears are quite delicate as they carefully pick flowers and berries with their lips.

September and October are very important months to British Columbia's coastal bears. Many thousands of salmon are returning from the sea and are migrating back to spawn in the streams and rivers where they were hatched. Coastal bears depend almost entirely on the salmon to survive their winter denning. The bears eat from dawn to dusk, consuming about 20,000 calories every day to build up layers of fat for nutrition and to thicken their coats for warmth in preparation for their long hibernation. They can gain more than twenty kilograms (40 lb.) in a few weeks, but will lose 30 to 40 percent of their body weight during the long sleep.

Photo: Bill Henderson

Photo: Wayne McCrory

Photo: Frank Ridler

All bears are intelligent and curious. They investigate any possible food source, learn quickly, can remember the location of a good source and return to it after many years. Bears are omnivores—they will eat both plants and animals.

Photo: Sue & Jeff Turner

Bears eat and graze constantly and are always on the move searching for "green salad" and berries; even the smallest insect is a treat. But for coastal bears, like the Spirit Bears, salmon are the most important part of their diet.

The Salmon Life Cycle

A female salmon lays from 2,500 to 8,000 eggs. While this may seem like a large number, only about one in every two to four thousand eggs hatches a salmon that will reach maturity and return to its spawning grounds from the ocean. The life journey of a salmon is a harsh one.

Once a fry is hatched, it can take as long as three years for the salmon (now called a smolt) to make it to the ocean. Depending on the species of salmon, the fish will spend from two to five years in the saltwater environment before it returns to its natal stream to spawn.

The fish are able to find their way back to their home through a process called imprinting. As the fry are on their way to the ocean, they record (imprint) all the odors and smells of their river journey. When they return from the ocean, they, in a sense, rewind the smells like a movie to retrace their original route. The salmon become battered and exhausted as they fight their way home and, as a result, often become an easy meal for the ever-opportunistic coastal bears.

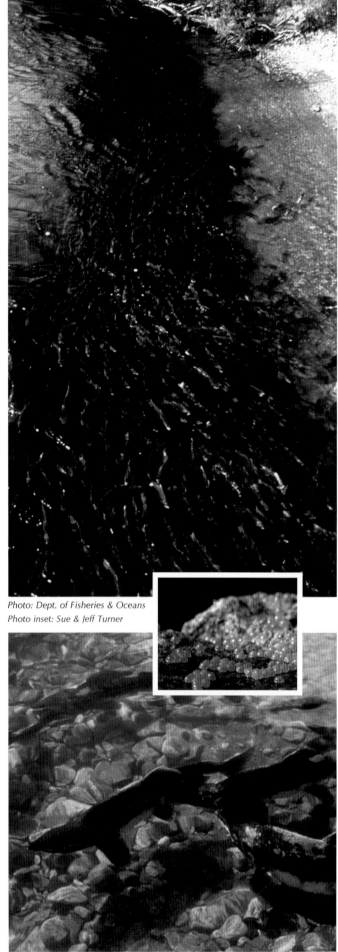

Photo: Dept. of Fisheries & Oceans
Photo inset: Sue & Jeff Turner

Photo: Erica Mallam

Photo: Dept. of Fisheries & Oceans

Pacific salmon spawn in autumn in freshwater streams and lakes. The eggs are left under the gravel of the river or lake bottom for the winter and then hatch in the spring.

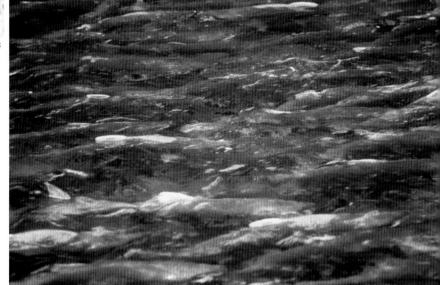

Photo: Dept. of Fisheries & Oceans

Newly hatched salmon, called fry, slowly make their way to the sea, which is where they do most of their growing.

Their years growing in the open ocean are filled with many dangers and hazards, such as fishing nets, killer whales, seals and eagles.

After a few years in the ocean, the salmon are big enough to spawn, so they return to their birth river system. They are able to locate their birthplace by smell. Now they must face the challenges of waterfalls and awaiting bears as they fight their way to their spawning beds.

Photo: Charlie Russell

Initially the bears catch some salmon before they spawn; but once spawned out, the dying salmon are easy prey.

Photo: Sue & Jeff Turner

40

Spirit Bears have been observed swimming and fishing underwater. Bears often gather below waterfalls to catch salmon; the fish are forced to slow down as they try to jump the falls. Often a leaping salmon is grabbed by a bear and becomes part of its dinner.

Sometimes the bear will carry this nourishing and rich meal into the forest to a safe place, away from larger bears who may want the food for themselves.

The remains of these rotting fish in the forest nourish the plants and insects. In streams the dead fish provide food for the new salmon fry.

Photos: Sue & Jeff Turner

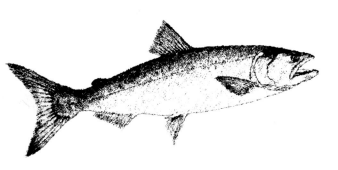

Hibernation

Unlike other hibernating animals, bears do not eliminate bodily wastes during their months of sleep. In other mammals, urea (containing nitrogen) must be eliminated in urine or it will build up to toxic levels, causing death. The waste products of bears, however, are broken down by the kidneys and liver into building blocks needed for the creation of proteins.

In all animals, including humans, living bones need daily exercise like standing or walking. This weight-bearing movement stimulates the production of more bone, which keeps the skeleton strong and flexible. After even a few days without exercise, bones start to lose calcium and phosphorous. Bedridden people, the elderly and astronauts in space (where there is no gravity) all experience bone loss. This loss causes bones to become thin and brittle, which results in easy breaks and poor healing.

The hibernating bear alone among all species on earth can go for two to six months while hardly moving and not lose any bone mass. The bear does lose calcium and phosphorous from its bones, but a hormone signal retrieves the lost minerals from the blood and replaces them into bone. Because of the bear's unique physiology, its hibernation is one of the most efficient and unusual survival mechanisms in the natural world.

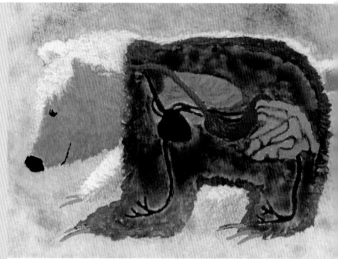

The bear's internal organs.   ©Liz Mitten Ryan

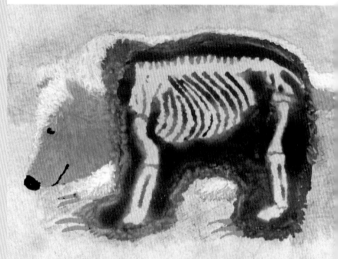

The bear's skeleton.   ©Liz Mitten Ryan

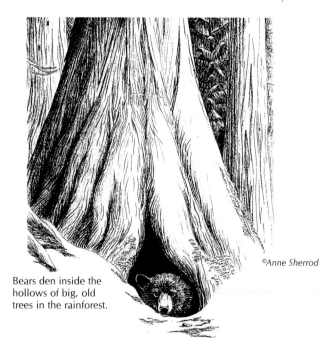

©Anne Sherrod

Bears den inside the hollows of big, old trees in the rainforest.

With the shorter days and the first snow of winter, the Spirit Bear enters its den for the long hibernation until spring.

The bear curls into a ball and within days its body functions change. Its heartbeat slows down, but the bear is kept warm by its heavy winter coat. It gets all the water and food energy it needs, about 4,000 calories a day, from its fat reserves. It gets protein from its muscles and by reprocessing its body waste products.

Protecting Bears and Their Habitat

It is illegal to kill the White Spirit Bears for sport — however, poaching continues. These unique creatures need an area like the proposed wilderness conservancy to ensure their continued survival.

Key Hunting Legislation Dates:

1924 . . .The government of B.C. banned hunting of White Spirit Bears.

1952 . . .Hunting of White Spirit Bears was reopened.

1965 . . .Legislation was passed to again ban hunting of Spirit Bears.

1993 . . .The government of B.C. banned trade in bear parts.

How Can We Protect Bears?

Support your conservation societies and urge the province to set aside more habitat. This preserves the homeland for bears, wolves, eagles and all the life of the forest and streams in the area.

Much of our land and sea are necessarily utilized by man for roads, housing, industry, logging, mining and hunting. It is essential that some areas are set aside for wildlife and wildlife viewing—only your concern will ensure this happens.

Photo: Wayne McCrory

Photo: Deloras Smith

Until recent times, the lives of Spirit Bears on the B.C. northwest coast remained peaceful, as Raven promised. The forest industry is a major employer in B.C. and was going to log much of Princess Royal Island. But in 1988 the

Proposed Spirit Bear Conservancy Area

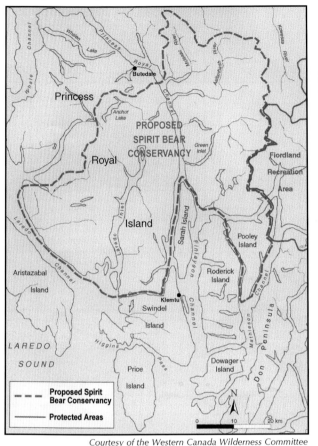

Courtesy of the Western Canada Wilderness Committee

Photos: Adrian Dorst

Valhalla Wilderness Society proposed a large sanctuary of 262,000 hectares (655,000 acres) and got a moratorium. Today, as a result of widespread public support and recommendations from First Nations and government Planning Tables about two thirds of the proposed conservancy area will be saved. However, this rainforest preserve must be fully legislated if it is to provide a true refuge for these unique bears, salmon and other plants and animals of the bioregion, and even more habitat, such as the magnificent Green Inlet, still needs to be protected. Logging policies in other areas drastically need to change to maintain other rainforest habitats cluding the irreplaceable ancient trees used for winter dens by

Photo: Frank Ridler

Spirit Bear Conservancy

Big trees and clean water are just a couple of the Spirit Bears' primal needs. Today there are many conservation groups fighting for the needs and rights of bears and other wildlife. By joining or writing these organizations you can make a difference.

For more information on the conservancy proposal contact:

Valhalla Wilderness Society
Box 329, New Denver, BC V0G 1S0
Tel: (250) 358-2333/Fax: (250) 358-7950
E-mail: vws@vws.org
Website: www.rmec.org/valhalla

Western Canada Wilderness Committee
227 Abbott St., Vancouver, BC V6B 2K7
Tel: (604) 683-8220/Fax: (604) 683-8229
E-mail: info@wildernesscommittee.org
Website: www.savespiritbear.org

Sierra Club of B.C.
576 Johnson St., 2nd floor
Victoria, BC V8W 1M3
Tel: (250) 386-5255/Fax: (250) 386-4453
E-mail: scbc@islandnet.com
Website: www.sierraclub.ca/bc

Write to your government leaders and the premier of B.C. to express your interest in preserving this wilderness home.

Photo: Wayne McCrory

Spirit Bears. If the Spirit Bear becomes the provincial symbol for the 2010 Winter Olympics, it is also critical for the government to fund ranger patrols in the new sanctuary and elsewhere to ensure bear viewing is low impact and to prevent poaching of white bears. It is up to us to continue to protect and care for wildlife based on kindness and common sense. Everywhere on this planet, our way of life should show a high regard for all creatures and ecosystems.

A Global Concern

Photo: Sue & Jeff Turner

If we eliminate our wilderness and wildlife what do we have left? We need to work together to preserve them. We must act with care and compassion. If the children and adults of today can learn to live in harmony with our wildlife and ecosystems, we can learn to save our planet for the generations of tomorrow. There is within every one of us the greatest force in the world that we must use—a spark of infinite goodness and a seed of good heart.

Kodie the Spirit Bear of Terrace

Photo: R.D. Anderson

Some years ago, a white bear living near Terrace, British Columbia, was hit by a car. The injured bear won the hearts of local residents and was named Kodie Kermode. Kodie was a friendly bear and became a household name around the town. This well-known bear died in 1994, but is remembered with much affection.

Kodie is now a Spirit Bear in the true meaning of the word, whose message is to teach about caring and sharing for all bears, especially for the rare and unique Moksgm'ol —White Bear.